My Future Life
Bullet-Point Journal

My Future Life
Bullet-Point Journal

Assess Your Life
and Plan for
the Future

LISA DYER

ARCTURUS

ARCTURUS

This edition published in 2022 by Arcturus Publishing Limited
26/27 Bickels Yard, 151–153 Bermondsey Street,
London SE1 3HA

Copyright © Arcturus Holdings Limited

Designed by Steve Flight

ISBN: 978-1-3988-1092-1
AD008855US

Printed in China

Contents

Introduction

Welcome to your #LifeGoals journal, which will help you put into action the goals you want to achieve in your life, now or in the next months or years. Here you will learn how to design your future by identifying what matters the most to you—not just the things you buy, accumulate, or what you believe others expect of you— and establishing and evaluating short-, medium- and long-term goals through a list-building tracker so you can create the happy, balanced, and fulfilling life you dream about. Combining self-help exercises with time-managed to-do lists, this journal will help you to uncover your true desires aligned to your value system and guide you through every area of life: home, family, relationships, health, wellbeing, career, money, education, adventure, and leisure time.

But just because it is written down doesn't mean it is set in stone: bullet journaling is about flexibility. Your goals will evolve as your life evolves; you will hit obstacles and find your way around them; your course may take a different turn or detour. The beauty of this journal is that you are encouraged to constantly re-evaluate your path and what is important to you and adjust accordingly, which will build resilience and adaptability. Hopefully you will find this book not only full of purposeful exercises but also an opportunity to explore your creativity.

Test out different letterings and drawing styles and add page decoration in the form of borders, boxes, patterns, and symbols. You may like to draw a sun for daytime and a moon for evening or night-time tasks or use washi tape or sticky notes to tab pages. There is no right way to bullet journal and you can introduce more artwork and design onto the pages or stick to list-building—it's up to you! Once you are underway, however, you should find that not only are you achieving goals that you haven't managed to reach before and you are becoming more organized, but you are less stressed in the process.

BENEFITS OF USING THE JOURNAL

- Helps you to evaluate what is important in life to you
- Empowers your decision-making and life choices
- Fosters resilience and self-confidence by building positive habits
- Encourages reflection and self-exploration
- Sets short-, medium- and long-term achievable goals
- Helps you visualize your goals and break them down into small steps
- Focuses on opportunities and roles that serve you and allows you to say no to those that don't

TIPS FOR JOURNALING

- Lay the groundwork by filling in the Q&As and brainstorming section first
- Start simply with achievable short-term goals
- Link your goal deadline to a life event, such as a birthday, work anniversary, or the new year.
- Make daily entry-writing a habit to be done at the same time each day
- Draw in pencil before you commit to permanent ink
- Customize your pages with decorative doodles
- Stick extra pages into this book if you need more space

Getting Started with #LifeGoals

To kickstart your life goal priorities, color in each of the categories below (which correspond to the chapters of the book) by rating your level of satisfaction with each from 1 to 10. Then start with the chapter for the category that needs the most attention! Do not try to overhaul all ten categories at once—you can probably only focus on a few categories at any one time.

GOAL SETTING
When setting your goals, be concrete about what needs to be done, where, who needs to be involved to get help you, and by when.

Throughout the book you will be encouraged to set a series of small goals with deadlines to get you to your overall final goal. Break these down into as much detail as you can and give yourself plenty of time to achieve each step.

Consider SMART goals. In 1981, George T. Doran, a consultant and former director of corporate planning for Washington Water Power Company, published a paper called "There's a SMART Way to Write Management's Goals and Objectives" in which he set out criteria to help people improve the chances of succeeding in accomplishing a goal.

LEVEL 10 LIFE

Chapter 1: **Home**										
Chapter 2: **Family**										
Chapter 3: **Relationship**										
Chapter 4: **Health**										
Chapter 5: **Career**										
Chapter 6: **Money**										
Chapter 7: **Leisure**										
Chapter 8: **Adventure**										
Chapter 9: **Learning**										
Chapter 10: **Wellbeing**										

Not enough time to do everything you want? Buy some time! Outsource chores you dislike—like, say, cleaning your house, walking the dog or washing your car—or hire a part-time housekeeper, chef or bookkeeper. It will cost you in monetary terms, but you could gain huge benefits in life happiness.

S—Specifics. Write in as much detail as you can about what you want or envision.

M—Measure it. Break it down into small achievable steps with individual goals.

A—Achieve. What skills or other people do you need to achieve this goal and how will you get those?

R—Relevance. Why do you want this and does it tie into your other goals cohesively and realistically? For example, you may want to live in a remote mountain region but you need reliable Wifi or easy access to specific supplies to do your job.

T—Timing. Be realistic about how long it will take and set deadlines accordingly.

TIME CHALLENGES

Short-term goals can be weekly, monthly or three-monthly. Start with these as you will get a much-needed boost of success when you can tick them off your list! Medium-term goals are likely to take you from six months to a year to accomplish and could be reliant on seasonal changes, for example, when you are planting a garden. Long-term goals are those that need a year or more to accomplish and involve bigger changes in your life, such as changing a career or moving home. Only focus on one or two of these at any one time and be realistic in what energy and time you have available.

Even with longer-term planning you may reach a crisis point where you have a lot to do in a short amount of time, due to unforeseen circumstances or a timeline that's changed. To help with this, time-block your tasks by breaking them down into short amounts of time to complete them. For example, in one eight-hour period you could devote 15 minutes to one job, 30 minutes to another, and so on. If you have more tasks than time available, go back and prioritize, migrating less-urgent tasks to another day. Then work through your daily task list setting a timer for each block of time.

Time Confetti

This is a term that describes unproductive multitasking, where those mundane tasks such as replying to an Instagram post or checking an alarm or fitness tracker, mount up to a collective fracturing of leisure time. In addition to the internet and smartphones intruding into our time, they guilt us into thinking we could always be using our time working. But if you spend all your allocated leisure time wrought with guilt that you're not being productive, you aren't actually relaxing at all. As explained by author and Harvard Business School professor Ashley Whillians: "Not only are we trying to fill our time with more work and being more productive, but also our time is more fragmented. We're more distracted, and that also contributes to these higher feelings of time stress." To counter time confetti, focus fully, mindfully and digital-freely on your task at hand—whether it's a conversation over dinner or a workout in the gym.

Planning Your Future Life

A life plan will help you identify where you want to be five, 10, 20, or more years from now. What are your long-term goals? How do you want to live your life? What are the things and values that are truly important to you, that probably won't change no matter how old you become?

Journaling is all about flexibility—and just because it is written down doesn't mean it is set in stone. Your goals will evolve as your life evolves, you will hit obstacles and find your way around them, your course may take a different turn or detour—the beauty is this journal allows you to re-evaluate where you are, where you are hoping to be and any changes along the way.

FUTURE LIFE PLANNER

Use the grids below to map out your longer-term goals. Don't feel as if you need to fill this out first; once you've worked your way through some of the exercises and goal plans throughout the journal, you may find that your ideas about your future start to crystallize.

IN ONE YEAR:

	GOAL	PURPOSE	OBSTACLES	ACTION PLAN
Home				
Family				
Relationship				
Health				
Career				
Money				
Leisure				
Adventure				
Learning				
Wellbeing				

IN FIVE YEARS:

	GOAL	PURPOSE	OBSTACLES	ACTION PLAN
Home				
Family				
Relationship				
Health				
Career				
Money				
Leisure				
Adventure				
Learning				
Wellbeing				

IN TEN YEARS:

	GOAL	PURPOSE	OBSTACLES	ACTION PLAN
Home				
Family				
Relationship				
Health				
Career				
Money				
Leisure				
Adventure				
Learning				
Wellbeing				

Supplies

For this journal you will need writing, drawing and coloring tools but as this is a guided practice, you may like to take your journaling further and invest in another notebook, as well as stickers, washi tape, ribbon markers or other decorative elements.

NOTEBOOKS

Dotted grids are the most versatile for creating geometric shapes, blocks, and lines, but you may prefer plain, graph, or lined. Numbered pages are useful if you want to create an index at the start of the journal. If you are doing a lot of coloring or painting, ensure you have appropriate paper thickness and quality so the colors do not bleed through the page.

PENS AND PENCILS

Graphite pencil for tracing out designs or lettering before finishing in permanent ink.

Colored pencils for delicate coloring and textures.

Technical drawing pens in black in sizes 01, 03, and 05 for fine artwork and writing.

Fineliners are available in many colors and sizes and don't bleed.

Gel pens come in metallics, neons, and many other colors.

Brushpens come in many colors too and are useful for calligraphy and watercolor effects. Some have a fine-tipped marker on the other end, or the set includes a blending pen.

Calligraphy pens for delicate scripts.

Sharpies for a punch of concentrated color.

Highlighters deliver a lighter wash in many colors.

Outline pens are double tipped in color with silver.

Watercolor pens have a water dispenser for different tonal color results.

OTHER

Clips for holding back pages.

Metal ruler—indispensable for drawing straight lines.

Tippex for painting out mistakes.

Washi tape can be written on and comes in many patterns and colors.

Double-sided tape for sticking down photos or creating "stickers."

Stencils, stamps and stickers are easy ways to add decoration

HAND LETTERING, TABS AND HEADINGS

To keep organized, decide on a style and font you want to use throughout for the headings at right. Choose a style such as script, lowercase, all block caps, or title case to denote different heading levels. Explore different font styles, calligraphy, dropped shadows, 3-D, and outline and practise the ones you like before committing to the journal.

a. Main headings
b. Goals
c. Steps
d. To-dos and Notes
e. Tabs (you can add these to the corners or edges of pages to group similar pages)
f. Banners (scrolls for headings) and decorative elements

Symbols and Signifiers

GRAPHIC DEVICES

Throughout the book you will see the below graphics which encourage you to assess your progress and write down any challenges or revelations along the way. Paths towards progress are rarely without some bends, U-turns or pauses along the way!

U-TURN: You took a step backwards. Identify specifically why things went wrong (boredom, illness, another priority, trying to do too much too quickly) and write down how you've dealt with the failure or setback.

DETOUR: Where did you go that you didn't plan in your step-building? Is this a new beginning or an opportunity to slow down your pace?

DREAM BOOSTER: Supercharge your goals by writing down a new idea or ways to transform this goal into an even bigger dream or objective. You could also power up your goal by setting two or three daily habits that aid in the progression towards your dream.

LIGHTNING BOLT: Take a risk here. Write down something you wouldn't ordinarily do that scares you, or you feel you aren't qualified for, but could also drive you and your goal forward.

CHECKLIST: Here are your to-dos that might fit in-between your steps, or important information or activities to jot down so you don't forget.

WAITING ROOM: Use this space for writing in things that can't go on your to-do or steps list because you are waiting for something, such as more information or the actions of another person.

 **REST BREAK:** You took a break. Here you will find a tip for enjoying a pause or getting back on track.

 STAR: You've reached your goal—Celebrate!

 **LOOK BACK/FORWARD:** Each chapter ends with an opportunity to look back and chart reflections, revelations and reviews of your journey so far, as well as what's next on the horizon.

COLOR AND SYMBOL CODES

You will be using marks and colors to denote various events and activities throughout the journal. You can add to the ones in the Symbols box below or substitute others you prefer. You place them before each task in the goal-setting sections and fill them in accordingly when they are progressing. Creating additional symbols, such as a dumbbell for working out, or an apple for healthy eating, helps you make a note quickly without having to write the word out, and see the subject at a glance rather than read.

Your symbols key or legend needs to be at the front of your journal so you can refer to it easily. It is a good idea to always associate colors to themes, so you can easily see all subjects referring to, say, health, throughout the journal.

Work out your color coding before you begin or else it can get very confusing!

Navigation Symbols
- ☐ Task
- ☑ Task in progress
- ■ Task completed
- ☒ Task cancelled
- ○ Event
- △ Make an appointment
- → Refer to to-do checklist
- ! Urgent
- ? Question—need more information

CHAPTER 1

Home

Home could be anywhere in the world you hang your hat or your forever home—it all depends on your personality, values, comfort level and ambitions. People are more mobile than ever before, and to some the home is more symbolic than a physical reality. This section will not only help you explore where you want to live and how, now and in the future, but also the more psychological aspects of what makes a home and how rooted you need to be to be happiest. Your home—and it could be an apartment in town, a house in the country, a boat or anything else—provides security, belonging, privacy, identity, and a place in the world that is yours. It can act as the one place where you have control in an uncertain world.

Goal Prompts

Here are some suggestions to help you think about your goals for your home life.

SHORT-TERM

- Decluttering a wardrobe
- Redecorating a bedroom
- Clearing out the attic
- Weekend DIY project

MEDIUM-TERM

- Creating a craft room/corner or home office
- Growing a vegetable patch
- Landscaping the garden
- Building a deck, pizza oven, or firepit

LONG-TERM

- Building an extension
- Converting an attic
- Moving house
- Buying a new home

Q&As

Q: Where is the location of your ideal residence? Maybe you are a city slicker longing for the beach, or you want to move to another country altogether.

A: . . . .

Q: What's your homebody factor? Are you happiest nesting at home or is it just a place to change your clothes on your way out the door again?

A: . . . .

Q: Which is the most important room in your home? Where do you spend the most time?

A: . . . .

Q: Where do you want to be on the property ladder and when?

A: . . . .

Q: What's your home decorating style? Traditional, mid-century modern, or hygge; extravagant, eccentric, or minimalist?

A: . . . .

Q: Do you enjoy hands-on home improvement projects? What would you contract out?

A: . . . .

Q: How do you use any space outside of your home—do you have a yard or outbuildings, a deck or hot tub?

A: . . . .

Q: Are you a clean freak or a hoarder? How organized are you and is your space working for you?

A: . . . .

Brainstorming Goals

To decide on the goals that really matter to you, think about the prompts and Q&As on the previous page, and your responses below, then write down goals—short-, medium-, and long-term—you have for your home in the mind map on the opposite page. They could be anything from buying a new sofa or hanging pictures to a major renovation.

EMOTIVE WORDS

Explore your feelings about what "home" means to you. Focus on how you want to feel before you think about what you want to physically have. Write down emotions, thoughts, and sensations—such as cozy, warm, squeaky clean, elegant, kid friendly, or show-room chic.

_____

_____

CLARIFY THE PURPOSE

What role does your home play in your life? Is it where you de-stress after work or a busy, humming place full of children and pets? Besides shelter, focus on what your home's primary purpose is.

_____

_____

IMAGINE YOUR PERFECT DAY AT HOME

What is your ideal day like at home? Who is there and what are you doing? What do you smell, taste, feel?

_____

_____

" MISSION STATEMENT

Now create a mission statement on what is important to you about your home. It could be "My home is my sanctuary / where all are welcome" or "My home is where I show off my personality." Any time you are unsure about what choices to make, come back to your mission statement to remind yourself of what really matters and whether your choices tie into this "home truth."

_____

_____

_____

_____ "

Life Goals

HOME

Your Dream Home

Draw your fantasy dream home, including the landscape and view, the road and the terrain. Really flesh out what it looks and feels like and use annotations to describe it in detail; for example, if there's a fireplace inside, there should be smoke coming out of the chimney.

Location: where in the world is it?

What's the sky and weather like?

Draw your house here. What style is it, how many storeys, and what materials is it constructed from?

Draw in the landscape and any special features—vegetation, plants, trees, mountains, or city streets, public buildings, animals.

Home Renovation

To get an idea of renovations or DIY projects you might want, or need, to do on your existing home—whether it's a weekend painting project or laying down new floors—fill in tasks or jobs to do in each room inside your home. Add your plans for your yard or outside area too.

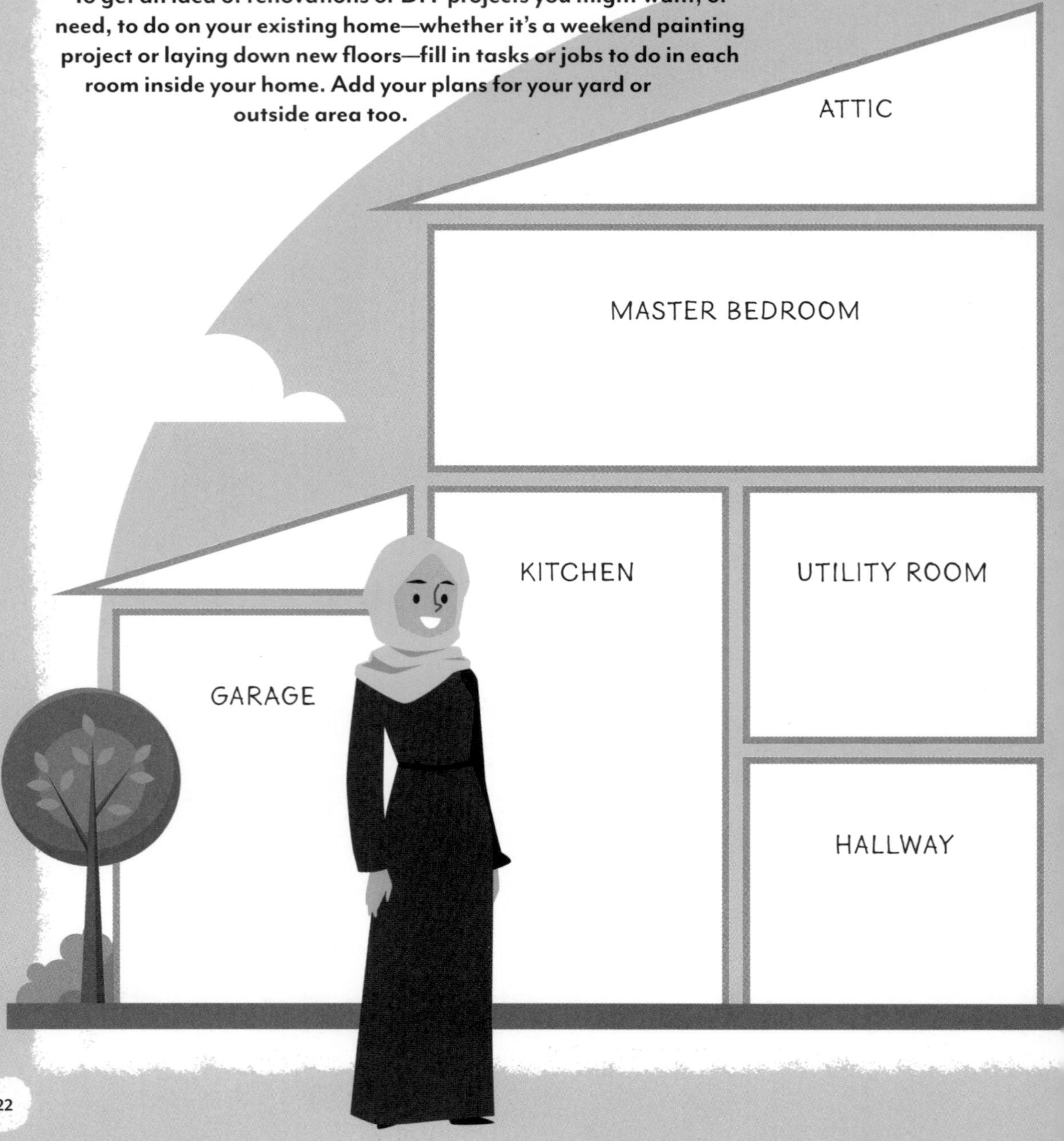

ATTIC

MASTER BEDROOM

KITCHEN

UTILITY ROOM

GARAGE

HALLWAY

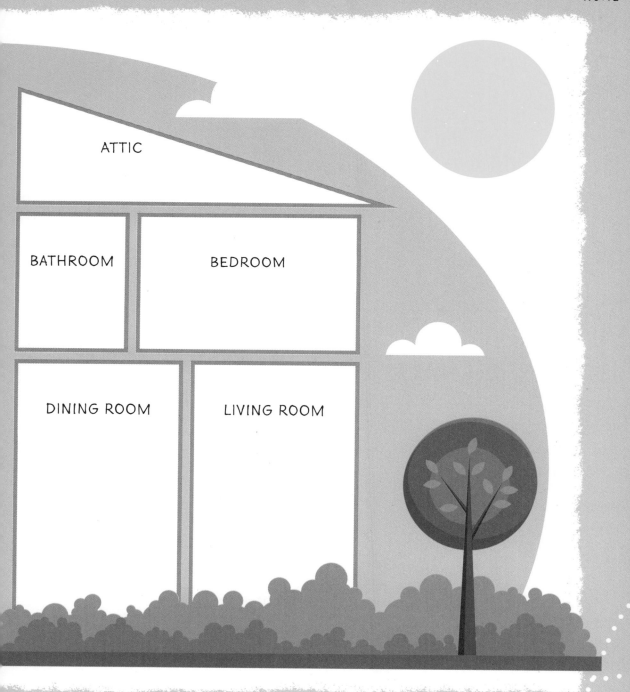

ATTIC

BATHROOM

BEDROOM

DINING ROOM

LIVING ROOM

Goal Tracker #1

Set a goal for the next week or month and plan every step you need with a scheduled date for completion.

STEP	DESCRIPTION	DATE
1		
2		
3		
4		
5		
6		
7		

Goal Tracker #2

Set a goal for the next one to three months and plan every
step you need with dates.

STEP	DESCRIPTION	DATE
1		
2		
3		
4		
5		
6		
8		
9		
10		

Goal Tracker #3

Set a goal for the next three to six months and plan every step you need with dates.

STEP	DESCRIPTION	DATE
1		
2		
3		
4		
5		
6		
7		
8		
9		
10		
11		
12		

You can't work at a 100% level 100% of the time. Take a breather to re-assess your progress. Step back and look at the big picture by reframing. Look at all the positives that have happened, rather than the things that haven't happened yet.

Goal Tracker #4

Set a goal for the next year and plan every step you need with dates.

STEP	DESCRIPTION	DATE
1		
2		
3		
4		
5		
6		
7		
8		
9		
10		
11		
12		

STEP	DESCRIPTION	DATE
13		
14		
15		
16		
17		
18		
19		
20		
21		
22		
23		
24		

Look Back

What went well and what didn't?

Which goals did you reach? How will you celebrate?!

_____

_____

_____

_____

What did you learn or are still learning?

_____

_____

_____

What's Next?

Write down a few new goals for your future here.

Have your goals changed at all along the way?

_____

_____

_____

_____

_____

CHAPTER 2

Family

What does family mean to you and what does it look like? Here you will set some steps towards that vision, whether it includes children, pets, and a partner, a blended family, your housemates, or a different family structure altogether. The questions here will encourage you to think about what you want for yourself now and in the future and will help you explore the health of your existing relationships. According to *mentalhealth.org*, people who are socially connected with their family and community live longer, are happier and physically healthier, while living in conflict or within a toxic relationship is more damaging than being alone. On the following pages you can set out goals for your family, whether that means repairing a relationship, bringing someone new into it, or dealing with a family challenge.

Goal Prompts

Here are some suggestions to help you think about your own goals.

SHORT-TERM

- Organize a weekly family activity, such as a games night or cooking a meal together
- Create a daily device-free time
- Make a regular weekly or monthly phone call to a relative
- Schedule a family circle— to discuss issues that arise during the week

MEDIUM-TERM

- Make a family yearbook of memories
- Create a family tree
- Volunteer for a charity or fundraise for a cause together
- Plan a camping trip or skiing weekend away

LONG-TERM

- Organize a family reunion for distant relations
- Plan a big celebration, such as a wedding, anniversary, or birthday
- Go on a long road trip, sea voyage, or globe-tripping holiday
- Add to the family— perhaps get a new dog!

Q&As

Q: What is your idea of family? Do you want marriage or a partner, children, pets?

A: . . . .

Q: How do you see your family growing? Who will be part of your family in five years, ten years, more?

A: . . . .

Q: How has your childhood informed what kind of family you want to create?

A: . . . .

Q: What family traditions do you enjoy and plan to continue?

A: . . . .

Q: What would you like to improve in your own family?

A: . . . .

Q: What do you do to have fun with your family? How often?

A: . . . .

Q: How much time do you set aside for meeting up with family members who don't live with you? Are there any obstacles?

A: . . . .

Q: Is there anyone in your family whom you've lost touch with?

A: . . . .

Brainstorming Goals

To decide on the goals that really matter to you, think about the Q&As on the previous page, and your answers below, then write down goals—short-, medium-, and long-term— you have for your family life in the mind map on the opposite page. They could involve hosting a family party, writing your ancestral story, or getting married.

EMOTIVE WORDS

Explore your current and honest feelings about what 'family' means to you. Write down any emotions, thoughts or sensations that arise for you—such as love, acceptance, legacy, tension, or duty.

_____

_____

CLARIFY THE PURPOSE

What importance does your family play in your life? Think about each individual member and their role in the family, for example the peacekeeper, the adventurer, the caregiver. What are the forces that join you together? What would you like to improve?

_____

_____

IMAGINE YOUR PERFECT DAY

What is your ideal day like with your family? What are you doing together? What do you smell, taste, feel?

_____

_____

_____

_____

" MISSION STATEMENT

Now create a mission statement on what is important to you about family life. It could be "My family is a place to find support and encouragement" or "My family respects everyone's unique personality and opinions." Any time you are unsure about what choices to make or hit a tricky patch, come back to this mission statement to remind yourself of these core values.

_____

_____

_____

_____

"

Life Goals

FAMILY

Family Tree

Finish drawing this family tree and fill in the branches. Start by labeling yourself on the tree trunk and branch out to your parents on the main two branches. Include significant people that are not relatives on additional branches, or draw them as birds, animals, flowers, fruit, or leaves on the tree.

"Call it a clan, call it a network, call it a tribe, call it a family. Whatever you call it, whoever you are, you need one."

Jane Howard, author

Goal Tracker #1

Set a goal for the next week or month and plan every step you need with a scheduled date for completion.

STEP	DESCRIPTION	DATE
1		
2		
3		
4		
5		
6		
7		

Goal Tracker #2

Set a goal for the next one to three months and plan every step you need with dates.

STEP	DESCRIPTION	DATE
1		
2		
3		
4		
5		
6		
8		
9		
10		

Goal Tracker #3

Set a goal for the next three to six months and plan every step you need with dates.

STEP	DESCRIPTION	DATE
1		
2		
3		
4		
5		
6		
7		
8		
9		
10		
11		
12		

✓ _____

↻ _____

If you are getting distracted from your goals by lots of unexpected tasks getting in the way, implement the two-minute rule. If you can do it in two minutes, get it done and move on. If not, add it to your to-do list for later.

Goal Tracker #4

Set a goal for the next year and plan every step you need with dates.

STEP	DESCRIPTION	DATE
1		
2		
3		
4		
5		
6		
7		
8		
9		
10		
11		
12		

STEP	DESCRIPTION	DATE
13		
14		
15		
16		
17		
18		
19		
20		
21		
22		
23		
24		

Look Back

What went well and what didn't?

Which goals did you reach? How will you celebrate?!

_____
_____
_____
_____
_____

What did you learn or are still learning?

_____
_____
_____
_____

What's Next?

Write down a few new goals for your future here.

_____
_____

Have your goals changed at all along the way?

_____
_____
_____
_____
_____

CHAPTER 3

Relationships

Relationships are the glue that hold our personal life together. Is there a romantic relationship or friendship that you'd like to repair or strengthen? Maybe you are not getting along with a roommate or colleague, or perhaps you are seeking your elusive soulmate. Investing in your personal relationships can pay deep dividends in overall happiness and connections. Relationships show us how to love, reflect ourselves back to us and help us grow, and support and encourage us in difficult times. Making your connections more regular and tracking the time you share with loved ones in your journal will help make them a natural and consistent part of your life. According to a 2021 report by Sheehan Fisher of Northwestern Medicine, healthy relationships result in less stress, quicker healing, healthier behaviours, greater purpose, and a longer life.

Goal Prompts

Here are some suggestions to help you think about your relationship goals.

SHORT-TERM

- Improve communication—better listening skills and better word choices
- Reconnect with a long-lost friend
- Find more quality time to hang out
- Surprise a friend or partner with a gift or event

MEDIUM-TERM

- Keep in touch more frequently with loved ones
- Make a new friend or foster deeper work friendships
- Join a local group or club to widen your social circle
- Organize regular date nights/social events

LONG-TERM

- Mend a broken relationship
- Find a long-term romantic partner
- Improve your physical relationship with your partner
- Make future plans together as a couple

Q&As

Q: What do you love best about your partner or best friend?

A: . . . .

Q: What special things do you like to do together?

A: . . . .

Q: What makes a good romantic relationship in your opinion?

A: . . . .

Q: What are the non-negotiables in your romantic relationship? Honesty, dependability, humour, fidelity?

A: . . . .

Q: What's your communication style?

A: . . . .

Q: How do you handle arguments?

A: . . . .

Q: Are your relationships equally balanced?

A: . . . .

Q: Do you see similarities in how you behave within different relationships; for example, are you always the instigator or the caretaker?

A: . . . .

Brainstorming Goals

To decide on the goals that really matter to you, think about the Q&As on the previous page, and your answers below, then write down goals—short-, medium-, and long-term—you have for your relationships (friendship, romantic, or both) in the mind map on the opposite page.

EMOTIVE WORDS

Explore your current and honest feelings about what your relationships mean to you, or what you want them to be. Write down any emotions, thoughts, or sensations that arise for you —such as happiness, support, stability, loneliness, or rejection.

CLARIFY THE PURPOSE

Think about your primary relationship. What role does it play in your life? Is it the most important thing or are you neglecting it? What are the dynamics like and are they serving you well? What would you like to improve?

IMAGINE YOUR PERFECT DAY

What is your ideal day like with your best friend or romantic partner? What are you doing together? What do you smell, taste, feel?

" MISSION STATEMENT

Now create a mission statement on what is important to you about your friendships/love life. It could be "My partner and I are guided by our common values and dreams" or "Just as I reach out to my friends when they need me, they are there for me." Any time you are finding difficulties, come back to this mission statement to remind yourself of these core values.

Life Goals

RELATIONSHIPS

Relationship Assessment

Think about your relationship dynamics. What are the things that bring you together and what drives you apart? Make a list in the boxes below.

STRENGTHS

WEAKNESSES

OBSTACLES/THREATS

OPPORTUNITIES

RELATIONSHIP LEVEL 10 CHART

Color in the level 1 to 10 for each category in your relationship—10 being the highest compatibility rating.

	1	2	3	4	5	6	7	8	9	10
Communication										
Time together										
Laughter										
Sex and intimacy										
Kindness										
Intellectual connection										
Future life goals										
Money										

Date Night Planner

OUR PERFECT DATE NIGHT
Describe your ideal date. If you've never had one, imagine what it would be.

_____

_____

_____

_____

_____

_____

NIGHT OUT IDEAS
List your favourite restaurants or new ones to try, sporting events to attend, and activities to do together—from art or pottery classes—to bowling or camping.

_____

_____

_____

_____

_____

_____

> *"Trust is the glue of life ... It's the foundational principle that holds all relationships—marriages, families and organizations of every kind—together."*
>
> Stephen Covey, author of *The Seven Habits of Highly Effective People*

Special Days Tracker

You'll never miss a birthday or anniversary with this handy tracker. Simply list the important dates with the name under each month and use it to keep in touch with your special people. You can track holidays and special days such as Earth Day, Valentine's Day, and Grandparents' Day, too.

DECEMBER

NOVEMBER

OCTOBER

SEPTEMBER

AUGUST

JULY

JANUARY

FEBRUARY

MARCH

APRIL

MAY

JUNE

Goal Tracker #1

Set a goal for the next week or month and plan every step you need with a scheduled date for completion.

STEP	DESCRIPTION	DATE
1		
2		
3		
4		
5		
6		
7		

Goal Tracker #2

Set a goal for the next one to three months and plan every
step you need with dates.

STEP	DESCRIPTION	DATE
1		
2		
3		
4		
5		
6		
8		
9		
10		

Goal Tracker #3

Set a goal for the next three to six months and plan every step you need with dates.

STEP	DESCRIPTION	DATE
1		
2		
3		
4		
5		
6		
7		
8		
9		
10		
11		
12		

Is conflict taking a toll on your relationship? Take time out to calm down, soothe hurt feelings, think about solutions, and acknowledge your own responsibility. You don't have to agree on everything. As long as the differences don't violate your values, try to accept that you may not be able to agree.

Goal Tracker #4

Set a goal for the next year and plan every step you need with dates.

STEP	DESCRIPTION	DATE
1		
2		
3		
4		
5		
6		
7		
8		
9		
10		
11		
12		

STEP	DESCRIPTION	DATE
13		
14		
15		
16		
17		
18		
19		
20		
21		
22		
23		
24		

Look Back

What went well and what didn't?

_____

_____

_____

_____

_____

What did you learn or are still learning?

_____

_____

_____

_____

Have your goals changed at all along the way?

_____

_____

_____

_____

_____

Which goals did you reach? How will you celebrate?!

_____

_____

_____

_____

_____

_____

_____

What's Next?

Write down a few new goals for your future here.

_____

_____

_____

_____

_____

_____

_____

CHAPTER 4

Health

From losing weight ,or quitting smoking and training for a marathon, to taking up yoga, here is where you can set your goals for a strong, healthy body. Journaling is the perfect way to monitor your nutrition, sleep, weight, exercise, medicine and ailments, and symptoms, as well as any triggers, allowing you to see patterns at a glance and take action over trouble areas. You might want to draw and track specific exercises, which is especially good for sports rehabilitation or physical therapy. Meal plans, shopping lists, and calorie counters can be created for diets, while any illness or therapies can be tracked alongside the treatments and results. The trackers will help you take control and responsibility over your physical health, not just in the coming weeks but for years to come.

Goal Prompts

Here are some suggestions to help you think about your own health goals.

SHORT-TERM

- Make 30 minutes of exercise a daily habit
- Sleep seven to eight hours each night
- Get outside in nature every day
- Walk 10K steps a day

MEDIUM-TERM

- Eat a more plant-based diet
- Swap out sugar, coffee, fizzy drinks or gluten
- Try a new sport or activity
- Create time for morning or evening stretching or yoga

LONG-TERM

- Train for a marathon or other athletic event
- Lose weight or maintain a healthy weight
- Embark on a vegetarian or vegan diet
- Give up smoking, alcohol or any other bad habit

Q&As

Q: How important is physical health to you on a scale of 1 to 10?

A: . . . .

Q: What health concerns do you have?

A: . . . .

Q: What are the triggers that derail your exercise, diet, weight, and sleep goals?

A: . . . .

Q: What do you do when you feel like giving up on a health regime or healthy habit?

A: . . . .

Q: What actions do you take to support your stress and energy levels?

A: . . . .

Q: How well do you sleep and do you have a regular bedtime?

A: . . . .

Q: How motivated are you? What is your self-talk like?

A: . . . .

Q: What obstacles are standing in the way of a fitter, healthier you?

A: . . . .

Brainstorming Goals

To decide on the goals that really matter to you, think about the Q&As on the previous page, and your answers below, then write down the goals—short-, medium-, and long-term—you have for your health in the mind map on the opposite page. They could involve getting fit, losing weight, changing your diet, or conquering an addiction or bad habit.

EMOTIVE WORDS

Explore your current and honest feelings about what "health" and "fitness" means to you. Write down any emotions, thoughts or sensations that arise for you—such as a desire to look better, have more energy, be more disciplined, avoid illness.

CLARIFY THE PURPOSE

What role does your health play in your life? You might be a workaholic who neglects their physical health, good at working out but not getting enough sleep, or battling recurring coughs or colds. What needs improving?

IMAGINE YOUR OPTIMUM HEALTH

Think about a time when you felt in excellent health and full of energy and positivity. Be specific about how you felt. Use that memory for setting your goals and motivating yourself to fulfil them.

66 MISSION STATEMENT

Now create a mission statement on what is important to you about your health. It could be "I respect, value and care for my physical body." Any time you are unsure about what choices to make about your health, come back to this mission statement to remind yourself of your core values. 99

Life Goals

HEALTH

Daily Habit Tracker

Add your own categories to the tracker list started here. Color in the square in the log for every day you've achieved that goal and leave the square blank when you haven't. There are 21 days listed here to correspond to the 21/90 rule, which states that it takes 21 days to make a habit and 90 days to make it a permanent lifestyle change.

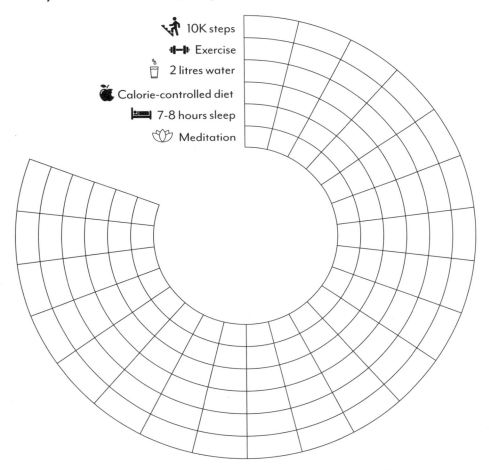

10K steps

Exercise

2 litres water

Calorie-controlled diet

7-8 hours sleep

Meditation

"Success is a few good habits repeated every day; failure is a few bad decisions repeated every day."

Jim Roh

PRE-SLEEP RITUAL

Listing your bedtime routine will help make it a habit for you
every night. Items could include: turning off your devices,
light yoga, relaxing bath, self-massage, skincare, herbal tea,
meditation, nature sounds, or gentle music.

*"Without health,
there is no happiness."*

Thomas Jefferson

1. . . . .

2. . . . .

3. . . . .

4. . . . .

5. . . . .

6. . . . .

7. . . . .

8. . . . .

9. . . . .

10. . . . .

DAILY INTENTION

To keep you motivated
and focused on your new
healthy daily habits, start
each day by repeating an
intention or affirmation.
Write yours here.

Goal Tracker #1

Set a goal for the next week or month and plan every step you need
with a scheduled date for completion.

STEP	DESCRIPTION	DATE
1		
2		
3		
4		
5		
6		
7		

Goal Tracker #2

Set a goal for the next one to three months and plan every
step you need with dates.

STEP	DESCRIPTION	DATE
1		
2		
3		
4		
5		
6		
8		
9		
10		

Goal Tracker #3

Set a goal for the next three to six months and plan every step you need with dates.

STEP	DESCRIPTION	DATE
1		
2		
3		
4		
5		
6		
7		
8		
9		
10		
11		
12		

You've derailed. Get back on track by using the momentum of your bad habits to substitute healthy alternatives. For example, if the first thing you do when you come home from work is open the fridge for a snack, substitute the habit by drinking a big glass of water, or turning on an exercise video first.

Goal Tracker #4

Set a goal for the next year and plan every step you need with dates.

STEP	DESCRIPTION	DATE
1		
2		
3		
4		
5		
6		
7		
8		
9		
10		
11		
12		

STEP	DESCRIPTION	DATE
13		
14		
15		
16		
17		
18		
19		
20		
21		
22		
23		
24		

Look Back

What went well and what didn't?

Which goals did you reach? How will you celebrate?!

What did you learn or are still learning?

What's Next?

Write down a few new goals for your future here.

Have your goals changed at all along the way?

CHAPTER 5:
Career

Are you passionate about your job, need a reboot, or would you like to try a new path? Here's how you can identify your strengths, skills, and innate talents and work toward a dream career or get that promotion. Whether you are looking to enhance productivity or time management, find a job, network with clients, track your work week, manage projects, or take notes during meetings, journaling can get you organized and keep you progressing towards your objectives. This chapter will help you brainstorm your priorities for your career and take the necessary steps to see them come to fruition, as well as help you think about any setbacks or missteps, or record wise advice you've received from colleagues and mentors.

Goal Prompts

Here are some suggestions to help you think about your own career goals.

SHORT-TERM

- Learn how to delegate
- Intern to gain experience in my field
- Go to networking events
- Be more organized

MEDIUM-TERM

- Earn an extra qualification
- Take an Excel or accounting course
- Improve my sales or productivity
- Win an award

LONG-TERM

- Get my dream job or make a career switch
- Start my own business
- Become an expert in my field
- Aim for FIRE: Financial Independence Retire Early

Q&As

Q: What is your idea of a work-life balance?

A: . . . .

Q: What does success mean to you?

A: . . . .

Q: What does fulfilment mean to you, and is that more, less, or equally important to money?

A: . . . .

Q: Is your chosen career matched to your personality and interests?

A: . . . .

Q: What are your talents and strengths?

A: . . . .

Q: What are your weaknesses? What skills do you need that you don't have yet?

A: . . . .

Q: Is there anyone that can help you reach your goals or mentor you?

A: . . . .

Q: Where do you want your career to be in five years, 10 years, 20 years?

A: . . . .

Brainstorming Goals

To decide on the goals that really matter to you, think about the Q&As on the previous page, and your answers below, then write down goals—short-, medium-, and long-term—you have for your career in the mind map on the opposite page. They could involve getting your foot in the door of your dream company, starting up a small business, getting a promotion, or changing career direction.

EMOTIVE WORDS

Explore your current and honest feelings about what "career" and "success" means to you. Write down any emotions, thoughts, or sensations that arise for you to explore associated values—such as creativity, entrepreneurship, teamwork, high salary, benefits, power.

CLARIFY THE PURPOSE

What role does your career have in your life? Consider the hours and location of where you want to work. Are you happiest in a traditional 9–5 office job or do you prefer working from home, having a couple of part-time jobs or a side hustle? What would you like to change about your current job?

IMAGINE YOUR PERFECT WORKDAY

What is your ideal day like at work? What are you doing and who are you with? What is the work environment like?

----

66 MISSION STATEMENT

Now create a mission statement on what is important to you about your career. It could be "I will start my own candle-making business this year, focused on selling and marketing via social media" or "I will pursue and complete a career change from teaching to law in the next three years." Any time you are unsure about your choices, objective, or progress, come back to this mission statement. 99

Life Goals

LIFE GOALS

Job Hunt

It is important to find a career that suits your personality and
values, and makes the most of your talents and skills. Make a list
in each of the boxes below.

EDUCATION

SKILLS

TALENTS

INTERESTS

"Find out what you like doing best, and get someone to pay you for doing it."

Katharine Whitehorn, journalist

VALUES

AREAS TO DEVELOP

WORK ENVIRONMENT

DEALBREAKERS

WHICH CAREER TYPE ARE YOU?

According to Lou Adler, the author of *Hire with Your Head and The Essential Guide for Hiring*, there are four types of workers. While every job and every worker has a mix of all four, one or two types will always be more dominant. Which are your dominant types?

1. **THINKERS** are the visionaries and strategists who produce the idea.
2. **BUILDERS** convert the idea into reality and implement it.
3. **IMPROVERS** make the idea or the system better.
4. **PRODUCERS** work in a repeatable manner to deliver goods and services to customers.

Goal Tracker #1

Set a goal for the next week or month and plan every step you need
with a scheduled date for completion.

STEP	DESCRIPTION	DATE
1		
2		
3		
4		
5		
6		
7		

Goal Tracker #2

Set a goal for the next one to three months and plan every step you need with dates.

STEP	DESCRIPTION	DATE
1		
2		
3		
4		
5		
6		
8		
9		
10		

Goal Tracker #3

Set a goal for the next three to six months and plan every step you need with dates.

STEP	DESCRIPTION	DATE
1		
2		
3		
4		
5		
6		
7		
8		
9		
10		
11		
12		

Embrace a false start. You may not get there on the first try but pause to reflect then keep in motion. Don't stop to wait for the perfect moment, for you to feel at the top of your game, or for the stars to align. Just keep your energy moving in the general direction.

Goal Tracker #4

Set a goal for the next year and plan every step you need with dates.

STEP	DESCRIPTION	DATE
1		
2		
3		
4		
5		
6		
7		
8		
9		
10		
11		
12		

STEP	DESCRIPTION	DATE
13		
14		
15		
16		
17		
18		
19		
20		
21		
22		
23		
24		

Look Back

What went well and what didn't?

Which goals did you reach? How will you celebrate?!

What did you learn or are still learning?

What's Next?

Write down a few new goals for your future here.

Have your goals changed at all along the way?

CHAPTER 6:
Money

From saving up for a holiday or car to putting money away for retirement, here you can set and track your financial goals from the short-term to the long. Use your goal-setting to make monthly budgets, pay off debt, keep on top of your cash flow, and change bad money-management habits. Even logging just one month of your incomings and outgoings can completely change your perspective about your money and where it goes, helping you visualize what you may otherwise consider an abstract concept. It will force you to honestly address any issues and helping you to make your money work better and build a more stable financial future.

Goal Prompts

Here are some suggestions to help you think about your own financial goals.

SHORT-TERM

- Create a monthly budget plan
- Spend less: stop buying expensive coffees or treats
- Always pay cash not credit
- Save for an emergency fund

MEDIUM-TERM

- Pay off a student debt or car payments
- Save for a wedding or international travel
- Put aside 10% of every pay cheque
- Plan for something fun and frivolous

LONG-TERM

- Save a nest egg for retirement
- Pay off your home mortgage
- Invest in shares or stock portfolio
- Buy a property-to-let or develop an extra income strand

Q&As

Q: What are your top financial worries?

A: ....

Q: What is the minimum amount of money you need to survive in your life? To thrive?

A: ....

Q: What did you learn about money from your parents—and which of these beliefs have you adopted as your own?

A: ....

Q: Do you spend money on things that really matter to you?

A: ....

Q: Do you live on less than you make?

A: ....

Q: Do you have anyone financially dependent on you?

A: ....

Q: Do you have any plans in place for paying off debt or for saving?

A: ....

Q: How do you feel about your financial situation?

A: ....

Brainstorming Goals

To decide on the goals that really matter to you, think about the Q&As on the previous page, and your answers below, then write down goals—short-, medium- and long-term—you have for your finances in the mind map on the opposite page. They could involve small cutbacks to your lifestyle, saving for a car or house, or seeing a financial planner about savings and investments.

EMOTIVE WORDS

Explore your current and honest feelings about what "money" means to you. Write down any emotions, thoughts or sensations that arise for you—such as fear, guilt, security.

_____

_____

CLARIFY THE PURPOSE

What role does money play in your life? Think about how you spend and save, what messages you've received around money and its importance, or unimportance.

_____

_____

_____

IMAGINE YOUR PERFECT SITUATION

Envision your ideal financial life. How much money would you need in the bank for you to feel safe and secure? What level of control are you exerting over your money?

_____

_____

_____

66 MISSION STATEMENT

Now create a mission statement on what is important to you about your career. It could be "I will start my own candle-making business this year, focused on selling and marketing via social media" or "I will pursue and complete a career change from teaching to law in the next three years." Any time you are unsure about your choices, objective or progress, come back to this mission statement.

_____

_____

_____

_____

_____ 99

Life Goals

MONEY

Building a Nest Egg

The first step to saving up for your future is: You've got to save money. It won't magically materialize later in life when you need it! To save up for a nest egg, emergency fund, mortgage, or some other big-ticket item, draw your objective (a big egg, a house), then draw a path to that objective. In each paving stone, write down a sum of money you need to build up to the overall total. Color in each paving stone as you achieve that level of savings.

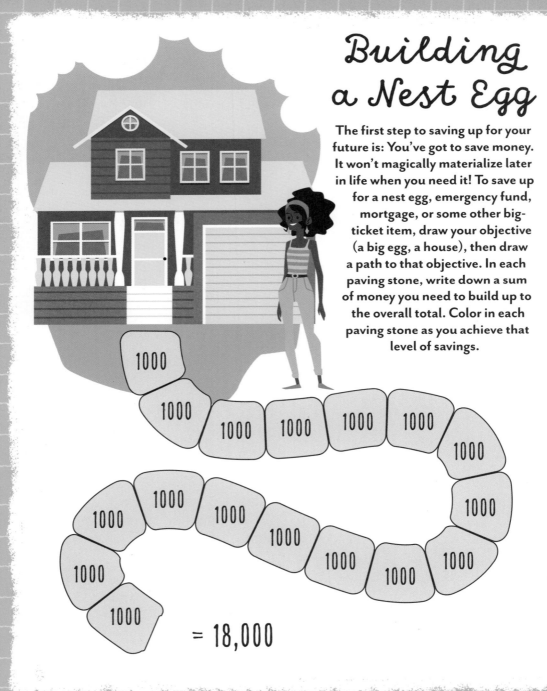

1000
1000
1000 1000 1000 1000
1000
1000
1000
1000 1000
1000
1000 1000
1000 1000 1000
1000
1000

= 18,000

SPECIAL SAVINGS

Another way to save for specific goals is to draw an envelope, as here. Label it with your goal, for example, "Trip to Rome," and fill the squares with amounts to tick off. When all your squares are filled—celebrate. You are going to Italy!

"Rule No.1: Never lose money.
Rule No.2: Never forget Rule No.1."

Warren Buffett

Goal Tracker #1

Set a goal for the next week or month and plan every step you need with a scheduled date for completion.

STEP	DESCRIPTION	DATE
1		
2		
3		
4		
5		
6		
7		

Goal Tracker #2

Set a goal for the next one to three months and plan every
step you need with dates.

STEP	DESCRIPTION	DATE
1		
2		
3		
4		
5		
6		
8		
9		
10		

Goal Tracker #3

Set a goal for the next three to six months and plan every step you need with dates.

STEP	DESCRIPTION	DATE
1		
2		
3		
4		
5		
6		
7		
8		
9		
10		
11		
12		

Not reaching your goals quickly enough? You might be trying to do too much. Take a pause and scale down. Strip away any complexity from your objective that makes it difficult to do and focus on a few simple and achievable money-saving goals for now.

Goal Tracker #4

Set a goal for the next year and plan every step you need with dates.

STEP	DESCRIPTION	DATE
1		
2		
3		
4		
5		
6		
7		
8		
9		
10		
11		
12		

STEP	DESCRIPTION	DATE
13		
14		
15		
16		
17		
18		
19		
20		
21		
22		
23		
24		

Look Back

What went well and what didn't?

_____

_____

_____

_____

_____

What did you learn or are still learning?

_____

_____

_____

Have your goals changed at all along the way?

_____

_____

_____

_____

_____

_____

Which goals did you reach? How will you celebrate?!

_____

_____

_____

_____

_____

_____

_____

What's Next?

Write down a few new goals for your future here.

_____

_____

_____

_____

_____

_____

_____

_____

_____

CHAPTER 7:
Leisure

How do you like to spend your free time? Perhaps you want to take up a new hobby, or spend more time with tennis-playing friends, or a nature-hiking group. Taking time off from work to have fun, pursue pleasure, and enjoy life allows you to switch off, rejuvenate, and connect with others. As a therapeutic activity, it can enhance health, happiness, wellbeing, and the quality and meaning of life. According to psychologists Tim Kasser and Kenneth Sheldon, "time affluence," or structuring your day so that you have lots of free time, benefits mental and physical health, and improves relationships, as well as supporting creativity and allowing time for ideas and thoughts to "marinate" and reach their potential.

Goal Prompts

Here are some suggestions to help you think about your goals for your free time.

SHORT-TERM

- Schedule time for a creative hobby, such as gardening or crafting
- Read a book for 30 minutes a day
- Schedule in do-not-disturb "me" time
- Do nothing! Set time aside each day for just chilling

MEDIUM-TERM

- Plan a weekend away to a national park or nature reserve
- Join a club, such as tennis, amateur dramatics, birdwatching, or salsa dancing
- Make time for something that brings you joy
- Plan monthly outings to the theatre, opera, or an art gallery

LONG-TERM

- Spend weekends or summers as a camp counselor
- Make one of your hobbies into a part-time profession—become an amateur golfer, personal trainer, or teach surfing or yoga
- Coach your local school's football or netball team

Q&As

Q: How much free time do you allow yourself in your day or week?

A: ....

Q: What are your hobbies?

A: ....

Q: Do you prefer to spend your free time alone or with others?

A: ....

Q: How often do you spend time chatting to friends, family, or neighbours in a week?

A: ....

Q: If you had more spare time, what would you do with it?

A: ....

Q: Do you gravitate towards outdoor activities or indoor ones, sport, or cultural?

A: ....

Q: Are you ever worried about wasting time and not being productive?

A: ....

Q: How much of your time is spent on social media or gaming and how do you feel about that?

A: ....

Brainstorming Goals

To decide on the goals that really matter to you, think about the Q&As on the previous page, and your answers below, then write down goals—short-, medium-, and long-term— you have for your free time in the mind map on the opposite page. Make sure you include some truly relaxing goals, whether it's a regular movie hour or mediation break.

EMOTIVE WORDS

Explore your current and honest feelings about "play," "relaxation" or "free time." Write down any emotions, thoughts or sensations that arise—you may feel guilt—or frustration, excitement or relief.

_____

_____

CLARIFY THE PURPOSE

What role does recreation or free time play in your life? Perhaps you neglect this area of your life, or you fill it up with chores. Think about how you would like to rebalance this.

_____

_____

IMAGINE YOUR PERFECT DAY

What is your ideal day with nothing to do? Think about where you are, who you are with and what are you doing.

_____

_____

_____

" MISSION STATEMENT

Now create a mission statement on what is important to you about relaxation. It could be "I recognize my need to relax and I schedule in one hour of 'me' time every day." Any time you feel too busy, overcommitted, or burnt out, come back to this mission statement to remind yourself to take time out.

_____

_____

_____

_____

_____

"

Life Goals

LEISURE

Reading List

Keep track of the books you want to read. Once you've read it, add a short review and star rating out of five and label and color the book on the bookshelf.

RECOMMENDATIONS

FICTION

	TITLE	REVIEW	★★★★★
1			
2			
3			
4			
5			
6			
7			

NON-FICTION/BIOGRAPHY

	TITLE	REVIEW	★★★★★
1			
2			
3			
4			
5			
6			
7			

HEALTH AND SELF-HELP

TITLE	REVIEW	★★★★★
1		
2		
3		
4		
5		
6		
7		

BUSINESS

TITLE	REVIEW	★★★★★
1		
2		
3		
4		
5		
6		
7		

*"We don't stop playing because we grow old;
we grow old because we stop playing."*

George Bernard Shaw

Goal Tracker #1

Set a goal for the next week or month and plan every step you need
with a scheduled date for completion.

STEP	DESCRIPTION	DATE
1		
2		
3		
4		
5		
6		
7		

Goal Tracker #2

Set a goal for the next one to three months and plan every
step you need with dates.

STEP	DESCRIPTION	DATE
1		
2		
3		
4		
5		
6		
8		
9		
10		

Goal Tracker #3

Set a goal for the next three to six months and plan every step you need with dates.

STEP	DESCRIPTION	DATE
1		
2		
3		
4		
5		
6		
7		
8		
9		
10		
11		
12		

If you're feeling stuck or can't find time, change your environment, particularly if it's one that's dragging you back into chores. Being exposed to new surroundings will encourage you to do things differently. Take your book to a library or café; walk to a local tennis court to bounce around a few balls.

Goal Tracker #4

Set a goal for the next year and plan every step you need with dates.

STEP	DESCRIPTION	DATE
1		
2		
3		
4		
5		
6		
7		
8		
9		
10		
11		
12		

STEP	DESCRIPTION	DATE
13		
14		
15		
16		
17		
18		
19		
20		
21		
22		
23		
24		

≪ 👁 Look Back

What went well and what didn't?

★ Which goals did you reach? How will you celebrate?!

What did you learn or are still learning?

_____

👁 ≫ What's Next?

Write down a few new goals for your future here.

Have your goals changed at all along the way?

CHAPTER 8:

Adventure

Travel and bucket-list adventures are the theme of this chapter—here you can log your lifetime goals, whether they are backpacking around Europe, or climbing Mount Everest. But adventure doesn't have to be thrill-seeking, and everyone has a different sense of what it means. You might enjoy discovering foreign cultures or sampling exotic cuisines, while nothing short of heli-skiing or running with the bulls in Pamplona will suit others. In a 2018 Austrian trial, researchers found that even just one short-term vacation had "large, positive, and immediate effects on perceived stress, recovery, strain, and wellbeing" and the effects lasted for 30 to 45 days afterwards. New experiences not only get you out of your comfort zone and away from routine daily monotony, they create lasting memories and help you lead a richer and fuller life.

Goal Prompts

Here are some suggestions to help you think about your adventures and dreams.

SHORT-TERM

- Take a hot-air balloon or helicopter ride
- Try a food or activity you think you hate
- Attend a live TV show
- Take a themed road trip for the weekend; for example, visit all the beaches/cemeteries/roadside attractions between two points.

MEDIUM-TERM

- Try something that scares you—bungee jumping, skydiving, or scuba diving
- Travel solo to a foreign country
- Island-hop around Greece for a week or two
- Go off-grid, sleeping under the stars, hiking, and wild swimming

LONG-TERM

- Swim in the world's four major oceans
- Glacier-trek or dogsled in Alaska
- Attend a festival such as Holi in India, Burning Man in Nevada, or Carnival in Brazil
- Go on a wildlife safari to the Serengeti

Q&As

Q: How open are you to new experiences?

A: . . . .

Q: Do you like to do things with a tour group or take the road less traveled?

A: . . . .

Q: Would you prefer a holiday that is romantic, cultural, relaxing, or thrilling? Do you like roughing it a little or are you a luxury-stay-only traveller?

A: . . . .

Q: Are you spontaneous or do you like to plan activities well ahead?

A: . . . .

Q: What is the one thing you've always wanted to do, if money and responsibilities were no obstacles?

A: . . . .

Q: When you do something outside your comfort zone, how do you feel afterwards?

A: . . . .

Q: What was the most adventurous holiday you ever had?

A: . . . .

Q: What was the craziest thing you ever did while travelling?

A: . . . .

Brainstorming Goals

To decide on the goals that really matter to you, think about the Q&As on the previous page, and your answers below, then write down goals—short-, medium-, and long-term—you have for bringing more adventure into your life in the mind map on the opposite page. They don't need to involve exotic travel or lots of money.

EMOTIVE WORDS

Explore your current and honest feelings about what "adventure" means to you. Write down any emotions, thoughts or sensations that arise for you—such as danger, fear, fun, excitement.

CLARIFY THE PURPOSE

Do you make time for adventure, travel, and holidays in your life? Think about how you can organize your life to make more time to step outside of your comfort zone and embark on new activities that will broaden your horizons.

IMAGINE YOUR PERFECT HOLIDAY

What is your dream adventure? Where are you, what are you doing, with whom, and what do you smell, taste, feel?

" MISSION STATEMENT

Now create a mission statement on what is important to you about having adventures in life. It could be "My happiness, confidence, wisdom and perspective grow when I try new things." Any time you feel concerned about taking a risk or fear jumping in with both feet, come back to your statement.

Life Goals

ADVENTURE

Adventure Bucket List

List everything you ever wanted to do, no matter how unrealistic or crazy it may seem. Get specific: instead of "run a marathon," write "run the Great Wall marathon." If you like, make it time specific too—you could list "30 things to do before I am 30 [40, 50, 60]."

"The purpose of life is to live it, to taste experience to the utmost, to reach out eagerly and without fear for newer and richer experience."

Eleanor Roosevelt

Goal Tracker #1

Set a goal for the next week or month and plan every step you need
with a scheduled date for completion.

STEP	DESCRIPTION	DATE
1		
2		
3		
4		
5		
6		
7		

Goal Tracker #2

Set a goal for the next one to three months and plan every step you need with dates.

STEP	DESCRIPTION	DATE
1		
2		
3		
4		
5		
6		
8		
9		
10		

Goal Tracker #3

Set a goal for the next three to six months and plan every step you need with dates.

STEP	DESCRIPTION	DATE
1		
2		
3		
4		
5		
6		
7		
8		
9		
10		
11		
12		

Take a cheat day, or "duvet day." If you have created ambitious goals for yourself, you can easily get exhausted and burn out. Clearly lock in the start and end of the cheat time so you don't derail. The extra rest and relaxation will give you a much-needed boost.

Goal Tracker #4

Set a goal for the next year and plan every step you need with dates.

STEP	DESCRIPTION	DATE
1		
2		
3		
4		
5		
6		
7		
8		
9		
10		
11		
12		

STEP	DESCRIPTION	DATE
13		
14		
15		
16		
17		
18		
19		
20		
21		
22		
23		
24		

Look Back

What went well and what didn't?

Which goals did you reach? How will you celebrate?!

_____

_____

_____

_____

What did you learn or are still learning?

_____

_____

_____

What's Next?

Write down a few new goals for your future here.

Have your goals changed at all along the way?

_____

_____

_____

_____

_____

Learning

Education never stops in life and there is no age or time limit. Perhaps you've been thinking about boosting your knowledge and skills by taking up something new, or there may be goals you've put aside in the past that you'd like to re-ignite. These could include getting a certification, degree, or further education, learning a language or musical instrument, or re-training. On the following pages, you will discover how to take steps towards these goals, how to manage your time effectively to reach them and how to overcome challenges along the way. Not only will you broaden your skillset and develop your natural talents, you will gain in confidence, stimulate your brain health and learn more about yourself in the process.

Goal Prompts

Here are some suggestions to help you think about your own learning goals.

SHORT-TERM

- Build good study habits
- Schedule a weekend course in Photoshop or video-editing
- Take a creative writing course
- Sign up for a cooking class

MEDIUM-TERM

- Develop a new artistic skill, such as knitting or life-drawing
- Discover all about a different culture—the history, food, traditions, music
- Learn to drive a car or motorcycle
- Take up massage, reflexology, or aromatherapy

LONG-TERM

- Learn a foreign language
- Master a musical instrument, such as the piano or guitar
- Get a further degree, such as a Masters or PhD
- Become an armchair expert—on 1980s films or Broadway musicals; on Picasso's Blue Period or mid-century modern chairs

Q&As

Q: What kind of knowledge are you interested in? Academic subjects, hands-on projects, career skills, artistic, practical, or something else?

A: ....

Q: What type of a learner are you? Visual (spatial/reading), auditory (sound), or kinesthetic (tactile/doing)?

A: ....

Q: What is your attention span like?

A: ....

Q: What does it take to engage you, and keep you progressing?

A: ....

Q: Do you like learning things for learnings sake, for fun, to show off, or do you prefer a practical application?

A: ....

Q: Do you prefer the structure of a classroom or independent learning?

A: ....

Q: Do you tend to learn step by step or are you more directed by linking ideas and concepts?

A: ....

Brainstorming Goals

To decide on the goals that really matter to you, think about the Q&As on the previous page, and your answers below, then write down goals—short-, medium-, and long-term— you have for further learning in the mind map on the opposite page. They could be as simple as taking an art class to as intense as embarking on a law or business degree.

EMOTIVE WORDS

Explore your current and honest feelings about what "education" means to you. Write down any emotions, thoughts or sensations that arise for you—they could be apprehension or fear of failure, but equally excitement and self-discovery. Look out for specific associations, negatively or positively, you are carrying from your school days.

CLARIFY THE PURPOSE

What role does your learning play in your life? If you're a student, it will dominate your life, but it could also be something you are encouraged to do for your job or that you always wanted to learn. Think about the end result: what you want to achieve and when.

IMAGINE YOUR NEW SKILL

Envision yourself in full possession of your new skill. How do you feel when you have achieved it and how is it improving your life?

66 MISSION STATEMENT

Now create a mission statement on what is important to you about your education. It could be "I welcome new ideas, skills, and thoughts into my life and grow as a person as a result." Any time you are faltering or feel like giving up, come back to this mission statement.

Life Goals

LEARNING

Monthly Timetable

Use this tracker to log the time you've devoted each day to your new skill, whether it is study time, music practice, or a language class. You can use other colors for mealtimes, sleep hours, breaks, exercise, and so on. Use the key below to designate colors for each topic.

MONTH_____ YEAR_____

	AM							PM												AM				
	6	7	8	9	10	11	12	13	14	15	16	17	18	19	20	21	22	23	24	1	2	3	4	5
1																								
2																								
3																								
4																								
5																								
6																								
7																								
8																								
9																								
10																								
11																								
12																								
13																								
14																								
15																								
16																								

KEY

☐ STUDY/PRACTICE ☐ MEALS ☐ EXERCISE ☐ SLEEP ☐ BREAK

> *"Education is not preparation for life;*
> *education is life itself."*

John Dewey, philosopher and educational reformer

MONTH_____ YEAR_____

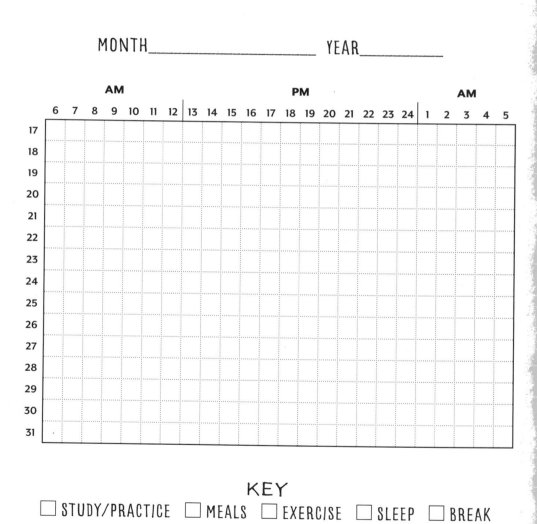

	AM							PM											AM				
	6	7	8	9	10	11	12	13	14	15	16	17	18	19	20	21	22	23	24	1	2	3	4	5

Rows: 17, 18, 19, 20, 21, 22, 23, 24, 25, 26, 27, 28, 29, 30, 31

KEY

☐ STUDY/PRACTICE ☐ MEALS ☐ EXERCISE ☐ SLEEP ☐ BREAK

Goal Tracker #1

Set a goal for the next week or month and plan every step you need with a scheduled date for completion.

STEP	DESCRIPTION	DATE
1		
2		
3		
4		
5		
6		
7		

Goal Tracker #2

Set a goal for the next one to three months and plan every
step you need with dates.

STEP	DESCRIPTION	DATE
1		
2		
3		
4		
5		
6		
8		
9		
10		

Goal Tracker #3

Set a goal for the next three to six months and plan every step you need with dates.

STEP	DESCRIPTION	DATE
1		
2		
3		
4		
5		
6		
7		
8		
9		
10		
11		
12		

If you are in danger of burning the candle at both ends, set boundaries to help you restore balance. Decide that you will not work past a certain time, or answer emails or calls in the evenings. Learn to say "no" to anything that isn't in your plan, for the time being anyway.

Goal Tracker #4

Set a goal for the next year and plan every step you need with dates.

STEP	DESCRIPTION	DATE
1		
2		
3		
4		
5		
6		
7		
8		
9		
10		
11		
12		

STEP	DESCRIPTION	DATE
13		
14		
15		
16		
17		
18		
19		
20		
21		
22		
23		
24		

Look Back

What went well and what didn't?

Which goals did you reach? How will you celebrate?!

What did you learn or are still learning?

What's Next?

Write down a few new goals for your future here.

Have your goals changed at all along the way?

CHAPTER 10

Wellbeing

Your attitude, mood, frame of mind, and emotional intelligence affect all areas of your life and contribute to your sense of happiness and fulfilment. You won't ever have time to put your wellbeing first, however, if you don't make the time, so here are some ways for you to fit specific self-care goals into your schedule so you can become the best person you can be. One size doesn't fit all, and you may want to focus on mental health issues or de-stressing, take time for your spiritual side, deal with messy emotions such as anger or sorrow, or devote more compassion and service to others. These pages will help you decide the priorities that will enhance and balance your life.

Goal Prompts

Here are some suggestions to help you think about your own wellbeing goals.

SHORT-TERM

- Do a random act of kindness
- Donate time or money to a charity
- Check in on a neighbour or friend
- Practice self-care by meditating or deep-breathing exercises

MEDIUM-TERM

- Explore your feelings in journaling
- Spend a week or more at a wellness retreat
- Join a mindfulness or empowerment group
- Put together a plan to manage stress and anxiety

LONG-TERM

- Book regular sessions with a therapist to maintain good mental health
- Attend an emotional management course, online or in person
- Volunteer at a food bank, homeless shelter, or charity shop
- Get involved in a civic, historical preservation, or environmental group

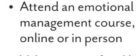

Q&As

Q: What makes you happiest and why?

A: ....

Q: What will you do today to bring yourself joy?

A: ....

Q: Where do you find inspiration?

A: ....

Q: What do you love most about yourself and what are you proud of?

A: ....

Q: What are you thankful for today?

A: ....

Q: Does the energy you receive in match the energy you put out or are you running on empty?

A: ....

Q: What are you doing to become a better "you?"

A: ....

Q: Would you change anything about your life right now, and what?

A: ....

Brainstorming Goals

To decide on the goals that really matter to you, think about the Q&As on the previous page, and your answers below, then write down goals—short-, medium-, and long-term— you have for your wellbeing in the mind map on the opposite page. They could involve greater motivation or discipline, better mood management, therapy, acts of kindness.

EMOTIVE WORDS

Explore your current and honest feelings about what "wellbeing" means to you and write down any words that spring to mind. What does it mean for you to feel well, to feel happy, to feel fulfilled? What feelings, thoughts, or external forces are stopping you from attaining this?

CLARIFY THE PURPOSE

What role does wellbeing and self-care play in your life? What are your objectives? Would you like to schedule in more time for specific things like cognitive behavioural therapy (CBT) or other alternative therapies, retreats or healing practices?

IMAGINE YOUR BLISS

What is your ideal state of being—energetic, elated, peaceful, content, fulfilled?—and where do you find meaning in life? Consider any spiritual or religious beliefs, and moral values that tie into this.

---

66 MISSION STATEMENT

Now create a mission statement on what is important to you about your wellbeing. It could be "I find happiness through my connection with others and being true to my self" or "I strive to make a positive difference to the world while I am here." Come back to this mission statement to remind yourself of your core values and purpose.

99

Life Goals

WELLBEING

Monthly Mood Tracker

Use these trackers to see how your feelings change through the course of a couple of months. Choose a color for each mood and fill in the tracker accordingly.

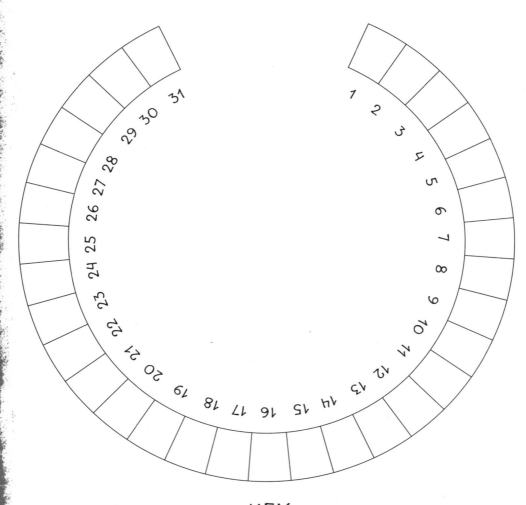

KEY

☐ HAPPY ☐ SAD ☐ DEPRESSED ☐ CALM ☐ ANXIOUS

☐ ANNOYED ☐ ANGRY ☐ SCARED ☐ BORED

"For everyone, wellbeing is a journey. The secret is committing to that journey and taking those first steps with hope and belief in yourself."

Deepak Chopra

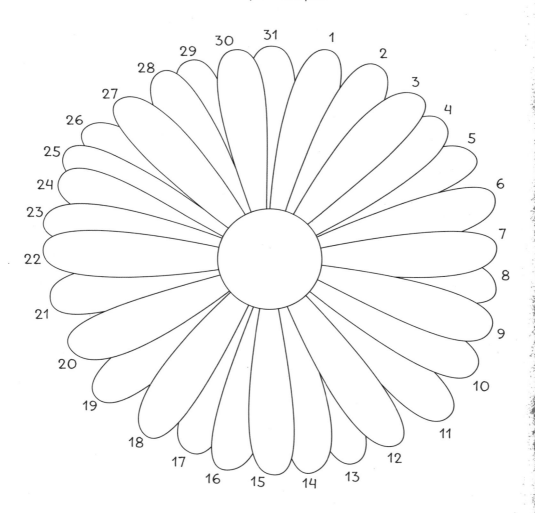

KEY

☐ HAPPY ☐ SAD ☐ DEPRESSED ☐ CALM ☐ ANXIOUS
☐ ANNOYED ☐ ANGRY ☐ SCARED ☐ BORED

Goal Tracker #1

Set a goal for the next week or month and plan every step you need
with a scheduled date for completion.

STEP	DESCRIPTION	DATE
1		
2		
3		
4		
5		
6		
7		

Goal Tracker #2

Set a goal for the next one to three months and plan every
step you need with dates.

STEP	DESCRIPTION	DATE
1		
2		
3		
4		
5		
6		
8		
9		
10		

Goal Tracker #3

Set a goal for the next three to six months and plan every step you need with dates.

STEP	DESCRIPTION	DATE
1		
2		
3		
4		
5		
6		
7		
8		
9		
10		
11		
12		

Take quick meditation breaks regularly throughout the day to re-energize. Stop and drop any time you are flagging, emotional, or unfocused. Just one minute of deep breathing through the nose with your eyes closed will calm your mind and clear your head.

Goal Tracker #4

Set a goal for the next year and plan every step you need with dates.

STEP	DESCRIPTION	DATE
1		
2		
3		
4		
5		
6		
7		
8		
9		
10		
11		
12		

STEP	DESCRIPTION	DATE
13		
14		
15		
16		
17		
18		
19		
20		
21		
22		
23		
24		

Look Back

What went well and what didn't?

Which goals did you reach? How will you celebrate?!

What did you learn or are still learning?

What's Next?

Write down a few new goals for your future here.

Have your goals changed at all along the way?

Acknowledgments

All images courtesy Shutterstock.